D1714808

silent h
as in ghost

Carey Molter

Consulting Editor Monica Marx, M.A./Reading Specialist

Publishing Company

Published by SandCastle™, an imprint of ABDO Publishing Company, 4940 Viking Drive, Edina, Minnesota 55435.

Printed in the United States.

Credits
Edited by: Pam Price
Curriculum Coordinator: Nancy Tuminelly
Cover and Interior Design and Production: Mighty Media
Photo Credits: BananaStock Ltd., Brand X Pictures, Eyewire Images, Hemera, PhotoDisc

Library of Congress Cataloging-in-Publication Data

Molter, Carey, 1973-
    Silent H as in ghost / Carey Molter.
        p. cm. -- (Silent letters)
    Includes index.
    Summary: Easy-to-read sentences introduce words that contain a silent "H," such as ghost, hour, and white.
    ISBN 1-59197-445-3
    1. English language--Consonants--Juvenile literature. [1. English language--Consonants.] I. Title.

PE1159.M655 2003
428.1--dc21
                                                        2003048128

SandCastle™ books are created by a professional team of educators, reading specialists, and content developers around five essential components that include phonemic awareness, phonics, vocabulary, text comprehension, and fluency. All books are written, reviewed, and leveled for guided reading, early intervention reading, and Accelerated Reader® programs and designed for use in shared, guided, and independent reading and writing activities to support a balanced approach to literacy instruction.

Let Us Know

After reading the book, SandCastle would like you to tell us your stories about reading. What is your favorite page? Was there something hard that you needed help with? Share the ups and downs of learning to read. We want to hear from you! To get posted on the ABDO Publishing Company Web site, send us e-mail at:

sandcastle@abdopub.com

SandCastle Level: Beginning

Silent-h Words

ghost

hour

school

whale

wheels

whistle

3

Jake pretends to be a ghost.

The whistle is white.

There are sixty minutes in one hour.

A whale is a mammal.

Mary works hard
in school.

Anna rides a bike with two wheels.

Where Is the White Whistle?

It's near the dancing ghost on the lawn!

Where is the whistle?

Did Sarah hide it in the thistle?

Did she hide it near the whale?
Did she hide it near the pail?
No, that is not the white whistle.

The white whistle is not
by the school.

The white whistle is not by the pool.

Sarah gave Rusty the answer.
Can't you see it?
It's near the ghostly dancer!

More Silent-h Words

honest

honor

rhyme

rhythm

what

when

where

whether

while

whine

why

Glossary

classmate	someone who is in the same class at school
ghost	the soul or spirit of a dead person that is believed to haunt people or places
map	an image that shows the details of an area
pail	bucket
thistle	a prickly plant with colorful flowers
whale	a large mammal that lives in the ocean
whistle	a device that makes a loud noise when you blow into it

About SandCastle™

A professional team of educators, reading specialists, and content developers created the SandCastle™ series to support young readers as they develop reading skills and strategies and increase their general knowledge. The SandCastle™ series has four levels that correspond to early literacy development in young children. The levels are provided to help teachers and parents select the appropriate books for young readers.

Emerging Readers
(no flags)

Beginning Readers
(1 flag)

Transitional Readers
(2 flags)

Fluent Readers
(3 flags)

These levels are meant only as a guide. All levels are subject to change.

To see a complete list of SandCastle™ books and other nonfiction titles from ABDO Publishing Company, visit **www.abdopub.com** or contact us at:

4940 Viking Drive, Edina, Minnesota 55435 • 1-800-800-1312 • fax: 1-952-831-1632